DARE

Do a somersault,
naked of course!

TRUTH

Do you regret having
sex with a certain
person? if yes, why ?

DARE

Lick your neighbor's ear

TRUTH

What is your biggest fantasy?

DARE

For 30s stick your ear
to your neighbor's
chest, then count his
heartbeat

TRUTH

Have you ever done a striptease for someone?

DARE

Improvise a love scene in which the boy and the girl give each other their first (movie) kiss.

TRUTH

Have you ever watched an "Adult" movie?

DARE

Pretend to have an orgasm

TRUTH

What's the strangest place you've ever had sex?

DARE

Spill something liquid on your neighbor's stomach and lick it

TRUTH

Have you ever had sex in public or in a public place?

DARE

Make 20 kisses
(where you want) on
the person of your
choice, he / she will
have to return them to
you afterwards.

TRUTH

Could you succumb to a sofa promotion?

DARE

Massage your
neighbor's feet

TRUTH

What's your biggest craziness?

DARE

Unclip your nearest neighbor's bra

TRUTH

What's your biggest shame?

DARE

Take off 2 clothes

TRUTH

Have you ever peed in
the pool / sea?

DARE

Kiss your neighbor's neck ten times and never in the same place

TRUTH

What part of your body are you most proud of?

DARE

Do a strip tease

TRUTH

What was your biggest drunk?

DARE

Do a lapdance

TRUTH

What does she prefer: boxer shorts, briefs, boxers, nude or latex thong?

DARE

Lower his fly with his teeth

TRUTH

What is the thing you hate most about a man?

DARE

Rub against your neighbor without using your hands

TRUTH

Could you have sex with another woman?

DARE

Be your neighbor's
slave for 15 minutes

TRUTH

Did you want me the
first time you saw me?

DARE

Your neighbor can do whatever he wants to you for 5 minutes and then you can do whatever you want to him for 5 minutes ...

TRUTH

What would you like to do with your neighbor that you never dared to ask me?

DARE

Mime the action you would like your neighbor to do next

TRUTH

Tell me about your best sexual experience

DARE

You have to show the tip of one of your buttocks so that your neighbor draws a smiley face on them

TRUTH

Tell us about your
worst sexual
experience.

DARE

Give your neighbor a hickey wherever they choose

TRUTH

Have you ever wanted to have a homosexual experience?

DARE

Swallow a piece of chocolate that was licked by your neighbor

TRUTH

Have you ever wanted to have a sexual experience together?

DARE

Your neighbor will auscultate you like a doctor for 30s. He will then make a diagnosis and prescribe an appropriate treatment.

TRUTH

What is the most sensitive area of your body?

DARE

Give a kiss on the breast / pectoral of your neighbor

TRUTH

Are you domineering
or submissive?

DARE

Kiss your neighbor's cheek

TRUTH

Do you like male stripteases? Have you ever seen any?

DARE

Kiss your neighbor's ear

TRUTH

What is your favorite
place to have sex?

DARE

Kiss your neighbor's belly

TRUTH

If you were a fan of sadomasochistic practices, what do you think would be the most exciting torture?

DARE

Kiss your neighbor's leg

TRUTH

The biggest shame of your life in bed?

DARE

Kiss your neighbor's butt

TRUTH

What's the most exciting place you've had sex?

DARE

Band your eyes,
undress, and try to get
dressed

TRUTH

How big is your penis?
of your breasts?

DARE

Put your hand in your neighbor's panties

TRUTH

When was the last time you masturbated?

DARE

Find a random porn video and act out a scene

TRUTH

Have you ever had a cumshot in class?

DARE

Take off a garment from your neighbor on the right with your teeth

TRUTH

What is your romantic fantasy?

DARE

Watch a porn movie
without sound and
mime the soundtrack

TRUTH

Where do you like to be touched?

DARE

Mime a blowjob

TRUTH

What part of your body
are you most proud
of?

DARE

What part of your body
are you most proud
of?

TRUTH

Have you ever had
sex in public?

DARE

You gotta give excited your neighbor on the right

TRUTH

Could you make love with your neighbor? If so, for how much?

DARE

You must say "Fuck Me" at the end of each sentence for 10 minutes, otherwise you take off a piece of clothing

TRUTH

Could you make love to advance your career?

DARE

Blind your eyes and you have to guess who is in front of you by touching him

TRUTH

Tell the hottest story
you have ever lived

DARE

Sit between your
neighbor's legs for 5
minutes

TRUTH

Have you ever been to
a Sex Shop?

DARE

Suck on food like a banana

TRUTH

What is it that makes
you crack?

DARE

Exchange clothes with your neighbor

TRUTH

Are you more of a thong? Panties? Boxer? Slip?

DARE

Take a picture of your private parts, and show a player 10 seconds

TRUTH

Have you ever had
sex with someone of
the same sex?

DARE

You have to run naked
outside for 3 minutes

TRUTH

Have you ever been
unfaithful?

DARE

Wedge your penis between your legs to look like a girl and show us!

TRUTH

Have you ever seen anyone here naked?

DARE

Feel your neighbor's buttocks

TRUTH

Have you ever had sex in your parents' bed?

DARE

Imagine an obscene poem

TRUTH

Have you ever paid for sex?

DARE

Mime your favorite position

TRUTH

Tell about your first time

DARE

Pretend to be in a relationship with a person designated by your neighbor on the left

TRUTH

Do you have any
regrets about your sex
life?

DARE

Kiss the foot of your neighbor on the right

TRUTH

Who did you think about during your last masturbation

DARE

Dry wood

TRUTH

Have you ever been a nudist?

DARE

Touch the chest of your neighbor on the left

TRUTH

What do you think
about swinging?

DARE

Give a 5-minute massage to your neighbor on the right

TRUTH

Could you watch your other half do it with someone else?

DARE

Be the slave of your neighbor on the left for 3 turns

TRUTH

Are you sweeter or brutal to the stake?

DARE

Take the hand of your neighbor on the left for 5 turns

TRUTH

Have you ever tried
sodomy?

DARE

Declare your laziness to the person in front of you

TRUTH

Show your favorite position

DARE

Everyone is changing
Places !!

TRUTH

Have you ever filmed sex?

DARE

Stroke your neighbor's nipple until it hardens

TRUTH

Have you ever done a nude?

DARE

Kiss your neighbor on
the left

TRUTH

What is your favorite
style of porn?

DARE

Caress your crotch for 3 laps

TRUTH

Have you ever been to a strip club?

DARE

Get topless!

TRUTH

Do you prefer to do it in the dark or in the light?

DARE

Suck the ear of your
neighbor on the left

TRUTH

Spit out or Swallow?

DARE

Do you know the Cremasterian Reflex? Googly and try it on your neighbor!

TRUTH

Rank your partners from the best to the worst!

DARE

Invent an action for your neighbor on the right!

TRUTH

Have you ever drunk being the driver?

DARE

Caress your neighbor
on the right

TRUTH

Have you ever slept with 2 people from the same family (not necessarily at the same time little rascal)?

DARE

Put whipped cream on
your neighbor's
stomach and eat it!

TRUTH

How would you like to sleep with your neighbor on the right?

DARE

Send a message to an ex!

TRUTH

Would you like to do a striptease to your neighbor on the left?

DARE

Caress yourself while
pretending to have fun

TRUTH

Have you had sex in
the last 24 hours?

DARE

Mime a 69 with your neighbor on the right

TRUTH

Have you ever slept with a really older person?

DARE

Kiss your neighbor on the right

TRUTH

Have you ever spied on someone in the shower?

DARE

Take off your Pants !

TRUTH

Have you ever slept with 2 people on the same day?

DARE

Everyone spanks you!

TRUTH

Have you ever faked
an orgasm?

DARE

Caress your neighbor
on the left

TRUTH

Have you ever seen a micropenis?

DARE

You are the BOSS!
Change the seats as
you want everyone!

TRUTH

Have you ever slept in disguise?

DARE

Put an ice cube in
your panties

TRUTH

Have you ever slept at your workplace?

DARE

Mimic sex between
snails

TRUTH

Have you ever known or been a fountain woman?

Printed in Great Britain
by Amazon

21611941R00088